DIGBETH

DIGBETH

NIGEL PARKER

The History Press

First published 2019

The History Press
The Mill, Brimscombe Port
Stroud, Gloucestershire, GL5 2QG
www.thehistorypress.co.uk

British Library Cataloguing in Publication Data.
A catalogue record for this book is available from the British Library.

ISBN 978 0 7509 8931 2

Typesetting and origination by The History Press
Printed in China

INTRODUCTION

For as long as I can remember, I've been a people-watcher. Humans fascinate me. From behaviour and demeanour to shapes and sizes, to the clothes they wear and the lines on their faces. Combine that with an active imagination and it's a great pastime. Where do they come from? What does that person do for a living? What kind of character will that child become? How has the glint in their eye developed? Or the furrowed brow or the distant stare? One place I used to frequent was a very busy pub. The landlord had been there for over 40 years and I would regularly wonder how many characters he must have seen pass through his pub and how easily and quickly he must have been able to divine their life in just one look.

Photography, and in particular street photography, must be a natural extension of people-watching – the human interacting with his or her environment. You capture so much in one frozen moment of time, and the fact that this tiny moment will now last forever makes it so much more profound.

I prefer to take candid street photos of people going about their daily business, usually with a wide-angle lens to show the environmental perspective too. Many of the shots in this book are taken quite close to the subject, but also show a good deal of their surrounding – I think it gives the observer more of an insight into who this person might be, why they are there, and what their lives might include.

I am a practicing osteopath of 20 years and therefore need to understand people as best I can. I have to glean as much information as I can a in a short introductory meeting one on one in the treatment room. How the person 'works' in both mind and body is an important thing to establish in order to decide how best to treat them. Street photography is a great balance for my treatment work – it's a path to understanding people in a relaxing and somewhat creative way. Observing the differences in how people of various shapes, sizes, ages and backgrounds move, in how they hold themselves and interact, is extremely valuable to me in this regard.

Whenever I leave the house, I've usually got a camera in tow and I'm always looking at the world with a photo in mind. I enjoy the excitement of what I might capture. When focused on street photography you need to see differently – looking ahead and seeing the photo before it has happened so you are ready to take the shot.

When I was 8 years old, I was given a camera and was instantly hooked. Shortly afterward I went along to a local camera club. A very nice old gentlemen from the club came round to our house and gave me an old, but still working, darkroom set-up: enlarger, photographic paper, trays and chemicals. Can you imagine the excitement of an 8-year-old taking photos and then blacking out the kitchen, watching the images come to life in the tray of developer fluid?

I've been a keen 'snapper' ever since, and a few years ago my love of photography was rekindled when I bought a new camera – a Fuji X100 – and I suddenly realised I loved street photography!

I was honoured when The History Press kindly asked if I would like to make a book of the street photographs I had taken around Birmingham and, in particular, Digbeth – an area now immortalised through the BBC's *Peaky Blinders* (and currently in the throes of HS2 railway development). The book has been good fun to produce, requiring some new photographic strategies and perspectives and getting me out of my usual comfort zone, which has been great for personal development and hopefully my street photography. I hope you enjoy.

Arrival. There are many ways to get to Digbeth, but one of the grandest is via Moor Street railway station, which has the iconic Selfridges store hard by. The station opened in 1909 and a later extension was built in 1930s style. It is now Birmingham's second busiest railway station

Looking up from Digbeth to the city centre, with the iconic cylindrical
high-rise 'Rotunda' building and the Bullring shopping area

Silhouetted walkers in St Martin's Square at the top of Digbeth

Legs

More legs. These are from the Custard Factory, which is located in the old industrial part of Digbeth on the site of the Bird's Custard factory. It has now been transformed into a community of shopping, creative businesses, cafes and bars

Happy chappy funking things up in the old railway arches of Digbeth

Digbeth Kitchen lunchtime shuffle

Gypsy fortune teller

Open Market

Opposite: Styling-it-up

Overleaf: Grand Central railway station (formerly New Street Station)

Unusual busker with an even more unusual helper

A cyclist passes a mural of Conroy Maddox, a painter from the 1930s Birmingham Surrealist movement and a member of the British Surrealist Group

Market lady

Opposite: Digbeth backstreet

Coy

The Connaught Bar, more colloquially known as 'The Point'

A couple of Irish old-timers who can't kick the nicotine (Bull Ring Tavern)

The Kerryman

Barber shop

New Model Army

TARDIS at the Custard Factory

The old Digbeth Coach Station, now the
National Express Coach Station, recently
refurbished from its former gloom

The coach station's refurbished facade

Opposite: The other entrance to Digbeth's coach station

Wandering through the coach station from the front

Waiting...

The coach station at night

Selfridges' distinctive disc-clad facade

Coach and driver reflected in the mirrored wall of Selfridges

The Afro-Caribbean community is heavily represented in Digbeth's Open Market

Market character

Market characters

The Bullring side of the market

Gypsy fortune teller

The fish counter

Eyes. One of the many graffiti works on the streets of Digbeth

Overleaf: St Martin's Square and church

Threads

The hand

Waiting for the drayman

St Martin's from the Bullring

A graffiti artist at the Digbeth Graffiti Festival, 2018

The inner part of the Custard Factory

The Barber's dog (Custard Factory)

Opposite: The skateboard shop in the Custard Factory

Overleaf: Lady in the indoor market (Rag Market)

Girl by the green pool (Custard Factory)

Opposite: Fig leaf giant, (*The Green Man*, Custard Factory)

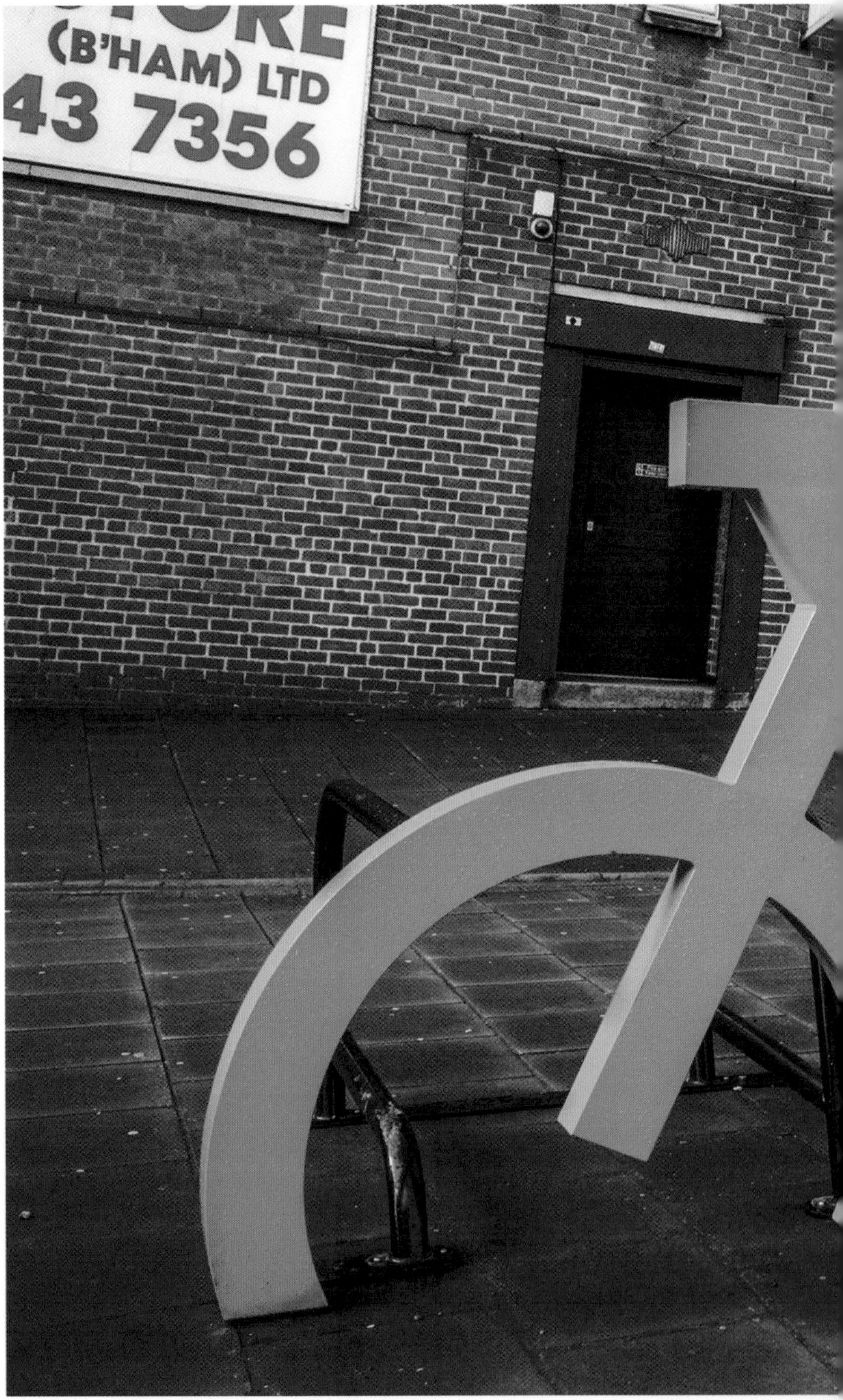
(B'HAM) LTD
43 7356

Checking out The Arch
art work at the rear of
the Custard Factory

Garrison Hotel art – *Peaky Blinders*-inspired

Fun photo shoot

Birmingham City University and Millennium Point

Greg of the Seven Sins Coffee Lounge
serving drinks in the Custard Factory